INSIDE THE STAR

THE ULTIMATE DALLAS COWBOYS FAN GUIDE

BY BARRY WILNER

First Edition
First Printing, 2019

Book design by Sarah Taplin
Cover design by Sarah Taplin
Photographs ©: James D. Smith/AP Images, cover (top right), cover (left), 42–43, 53, 61, 71; Chris Szagola/AP Images, cover (bottom right); Vernon Biever/AP Images, 4, 33, 47, 67, 77; David Durochik/AP Images, 7; AP Images, 9, 11, 12, 20, 30, 62, 84–85, 105; Ferd Kaufman/AP Images, 14; Arthur Anderson/AP Images, 17; Tony Tomsic/AP Images, 19, 28–29, 88; Rob Schumacher/AP Images, 23; Paul Spinelli/AP Images, 26; Fort Worth Star-Telegram/AP Images, 37, 39; Charles Bennett/AP Images, 44; Pat Sullivan/AP Images, 50–51; John Froschauer/AP Images, 54; Ron Jenkins/AP Images, 58; Alex Brandon/AP Images, 72; Eric Gay/AP Images, 74; Bill Kostroun/AP Images, 79, 97; Tony Gutierrez/AP Images, 82; Peter Read Miller/AP Images, 92; NFL Photos/AP Images, 94

Design Elements ©: Pixabay

Press Box Books, an imprint of Press Room Editions.

Library of Congress Control Number: 2018952196

ISBN:
978-1-63494-058-0 (paperback)
978-1-63494-070-2 (epub)
978-1-63494-082-5 (hosted ebook)

Distributed by North Star Editions, Inc.
2297 Waters Drive
Mendota Heights, MN 55120
www.northstareditions.com

Printed in the United States of America

TABLE OF CONTENTS

CHAPTER 1

HAIL MARY

Roger Staubach is famous for many things. As the greatest quarterback in Naval Academy history, he won the Heisman Trophy in 1963. Then, after serving four years in the military, he joined the Dallas Cowboys. He went from backup to starter to champion to Hall of Famer. Dallas won two Super Bowls with Staubach at the helm, and he made the NFL's All-Decade team for the 1970s.

Despite all those achievements, people always seem to ask Staubach about one play. And one phrase: Hail Mary.

The same goes for Drew Pearson, a star receiver for the Cowboys in the 1970s and also a member of the All-Decade team.

Roger Staubach and the Cowboys faced relentless pressure from the Vikings during their 1975 playoff game.

"It slowly became the term for anybody that was kind of in trouble, and you had a hope," Staubach said years later. "Now the Hail Mary is used for politics, for business, and for football."

Especially for football, where every desperation pass by a losing team at the end of a game is described the same way: Hail Mary.

"I get asked almost every day about the Hail Mary," Pearson said. "In some way, shape, or form, people ask me about that. To this day, when I sign autographs I write 'Hail Mary always' or 'Hail Mary to you,' 'Hail Mary wishes,' things like that."

So what prompted the phrase?

The Cowboys were visiting the Minnesota Vikings on December 28, 1975, for a playoff game. Dallas was a wild-card team with a 10–4 record. The Vikings, meanwhile, were a powerhouse. They had won the NFC Central with a 12–2 record, which was tied for best in the league.

The game took place at frigid Metropolitan Stadium, where the wind chill was only 17 degrees Fahrenheit. The Cowboys took a 10–7 lead early in the fourth quarter. But then Minnesota went in front 14–10, and things started to look bleak for Dallas.

Vikings defensive end Jim Marshall, a member of the Purple People Eaters, tackles Staubach.

Facing second-and-10 with less than 30 seconds remaining in the game, Staubach dropped back to pass against the Purple People Eaters. That was the nickname for the tough Vikings defense, which had allowed an average of only 13 points per game during the regular season. Along with a fierce pass rush, the Vikings also had a future Hall of Fame safety in Paul Krause. Staubach knew he had to keep Krause from double-covering Pearson.

"I pumped and looked Krause off," Staubach explained. "He really should have helped."

Instead, Krause covered Cowboys receiver Golden Richards while Pearson sprinted down the right sideline against cornerback Nate Wright.

The fans in Minnesota may have been cold, but they weren't too frozen to cheer loudly as Staubach heaved the ball in desperation. After all, what chance did Dallas have for a miracle finish against that awesome defense?

Plenty, it turned out—even on a slippery field at the end of a tiring contest.

"I had one more gear left," Pearson said. "If Roger had thrown it to the back of the end zone, I could have shifted into that last gear, done the toe dance in the back of the end zone, and walked away untouched."

But the pass was a few yards short of the end zone. Pearson slowed, as did Wright. They bumped into each other, and Wright stumbled as Pearson grabbed the pass.

"As I looked back and saw the ball coming," Pearson said, "I saw it was going to be short, and then I did that swim move to get inside position. In doing that, I made contact with Nate, but there was no deliberate

Cowboys receiver Drew Pearson runs into the end zone after catching a Hail Mary pass from Roger Staubach.

push. With that contact, he went down and I was able to swing my arms around.

"The ball hit my hands as I brought them around, and it went through my hands. I ended up catching the Hail Mary with my elbow and my hip. . . . That adds to the mystique and aura of the Hail Mary."

So does the claim–by Vikings players and their fans–that Pearson pushed off and should have been called for offensive pass interference.

Nonetheless, Pearson caught the ball with 24 seconds left and shimmied into the end zone for a

DREW PEARSON

On the list of great Cowboys receivers, Drew Pearson must be near the top. His Hail Mary catch was just one of many big-time plays during an impressive career.

In college, Pearson was a quarterback at Tulsa before becoming a wide receiver. He was raw at the position when he joined the Cowboys, but he soon blossomed into a No. 1 pass catcher. Twice he gained more than 1,000 yards receiving. And in 1977, he led the NFL in receiving yards.

During his career, Pearson caught 48 touchdown passes in the regular season and eight more in the playoffs. He entered the Cowboys Ring of Honor in 2011.

17–14 win. Oddly, the famous football didn't become Pearson's souvenir. In celebration, he threw it over the stands and into the parking lot.

The winning ball may be long gone. But thanks to Pearson and Staubach's heroics, *Hail Mary* became a permanent football term.

"When they asked me about it, I think the actual quote was, 'Well, I guess you could call it a Hail Mary. You throw it up and pray,'" Staubach said. "I could have

Staubach remains calm under pressure during a 1975 playoff game in Minnesota.

said 'Our Father' or 'Glory Be.' But I don't think 'Our Father' would have carried on."

The Hail Mary has become a common play in today's NFL. Just about any time a team is trailing with time for one last play, the quarterback will heave a desperate pass down the field. No Hail Mary, however, can compare to the first one.

"The preparation to defend for the Hail Mary is different," Staubach said. "Today, teams work on it. When Drew caught it, there wasn't anybody else there."

CHAPTER 2

AMERICA'S TEAM

Once in a while, a group of US athletes becomes known as America's Team. The 1980 Olympic hockey team, for example, scored one of the biggest upsets in sports history against the Soviet Union. And in the 1999 Women's World Cup, the champion US team became pioneers for the game of soccer. But in most people's minds, there's only one America's Team: the Dallas Cowboys.

But where did that nickname come from? And does it really apply?

Bob Ryan, an editor at NFL Films, coined the phrase. Ryan knew that the Cowboys were popular not just in Texas but also across the United States. After all, they were one of the league's most successful teams at the time. So when he was working on the

Players carry Cowboys head coach Tom Landry off the field after the team's victory in Super Bowl XII.

Cowboys president Tex Schramm poses with the Lombardi Trophy in 1977.

team's 1978 highlight film, he suggested that it should be titled "America's Team."

Cowboys president Tex Schramm loved the idea. The team's coaches and players didn't. More on that later.

"(The Cowboys) had legions of fans across the country," Ryan said. "They were a team that you either loved or hated. They were like Notre Dame, the Yankees, the Celtics, those kinds of teams that drew

TEX SCHRAMM

Early in his career, Tex Schramm worked in a number of jobs including publicity and television. But he made his mark as president and general manager of the Cowboys from their beginning in 1960. During Schramm's 29 seasons, Dallas made five Super Bowls, with two wins. The Cowboys also went 20 straight seasons with a winning record.

Schramm played a number of important roles, not just for the Cowboys but for the entire league. He was one of the NFL's rule-makers. He helped NFL Commissioner Pete Rozelle with TV contracts. He came up with the lineup of three divisions in each conference (now four). He pushed for video instant replay to help referees make calls.

By the time Schramm left the Cowboys in 1989, his legacy was undeniable. In 1991 Schramm was inducted into the Pro Football Hall of Fame.

large numbers in ratings because of that love-hate relationship. If there was a national team in pro football, there was only one team, and that was the Dallas Cowboys."

The name stuck. And decades later, it still fits. The Cowboys are the most valuable franchise in any sport, worth more than $4 billion according to *Forbes* magazine. They also sell the most jerseys and souvenirs of any NFL team. And the Cowboys tend to draw the biggest TV audiences, especially when they're winning.

It doesn't hurt that the Cowboys have a magnificent home stadium where many other major sporting events occur. Or that owner Jerry Jones is one of the most powerful people in football. Or that their logo, the star, is . . . well, star-worthy.

Schramm had a knack for drawing up interest in the Cowboys. It was his idea, for example, to have the Cowboys play each year on Thanksgiving. That game puts the team in the national spotlight. A classic nickname like America's Team could only help grow the brand. But while Schramm may have smiled when he first heard the nickname, coach Tom Landry and the guys on the field shuddered.

"Wherever we went," said quarterback Roger Staubach, "people were always giving us a hard time."

The Cowboys were on the road playing the Philadelphia Eagles shortly after the nickname caught on. During one play, Staubach took a hard tackle from Eagles defender Bill Bergey. "I kind of got the wind

Cowboys running back Tony Dorsett is tackled during a 1979 game, shortly after the nickname America's Team caught on.

knocked out of me," Staubach said. "I'm laying there. Bergey comes over and grabs my hand, and he pulls me up and he says, 'Take that, America's quarterback.'"

That's when Staubach realized the name wasn't too popular with players on other teams.

"I like it today, because I was proud of being part of America's Team," Staubach said. "But when we were playing, it was bad enough playing the other guys, but

GIL BRANDT

For nearly 30 years, Gil Brandt was the guy who found the talent for the Cowboys. He oversaw the team's scouting, often visiting college practices and games himself. He made sure the Cowboys knew something about every player eligible for the draft each year, and much of that information was carried in his head. Brandt seemed to remember everything, from which high school a player attended to what his parents did for a living.

Brandt was also a pioneer. Early in his tenure, the Cowboys became one of the first sports franchises to use computers. Dallas was also the first NFL team to look for players from other sports.

After leaving the Cowboys, Brandt worked as a draft expert for the NFL. He also worked as a radio analyst. Thanks to his important contributions to the game, Brandt is known as the Godfather of Scouting.

when they thought we were kind of shoving it in their face with America's Team, I don't think as players we were crazy about it."

Gil Brandt, who helped build the team from day one, believes he knows the secret formula for America's Team.

Gil Brandt served as the Cowboys' vice president of personnel from 1960 to 1988.

"We did a lot of things people didn't really realize we did," said Brandt, the team's first player personnel director. "We answered every letter from every fan, and we would put a little flyer in there that they could buy T-shirts for $4 and wristbands for $2 and so forth. Everybody was surprised that they would actually get a letter from an NFL team."

All that work paid off. "I think we're probably into the grandkids of those people we started with," Brandt said.

APEX
COWBOYS

CHAPTER 3

JERRY AND JIMMY

Jerry Jones and Jimmy Johnson first met in the 1960s, when they were teammates on the University of Arkansas football team. After college, the two men went their separate ways. Jones made a fortune in the oil business, while Johnson became a top football coach at Oklahoma State University and later at the University of Miami.

Then in 1989, Jones bought the Dallas Cowboys. One of his first decisions was to hire Johnson as head coach. That meant Jones was firing Tom Landry, the only coach in franchise history and a man heading to the Hall of Fame. It wasn't a popular move, and Jones later regretted the way he handled it.

"If I had a chance to do it over again, I would've waited a year and just got my feet on the ground a

Jimmy Johnson calls a play during a 1993 playoff game against the Eagles.

little bit more," Jones said, "and probably just gone with the staff that we had and then later made the ultimate change that I made."

But the Cowboys were now under the control of the two J.J.s–the owner and the coach. Jones also served as the team's general manager, meaning he would have final say over trades and draft picks.

Still, it was Johnson who was the wheeler-dealer. And boy, could he make moves: 51 trades in all. The biggest one, which occurred in 1989, wound up turning the Cowboys from a pathetic 1–15 team into a champion.

"When I told Jerry that we were going to trade Herschel Walker, he was kind of astonished," Johnson said. He planned to send the star running back–by far the Cowboys' best player–to Minnesota.

"(Jones) said, 'Really? You can't get rid of Herschel Walker. We won't score a point if we don't have Herschel Walker.' And that's what Minnesota thought. Minnesota thought, 'This college guy, we'll pull one over on him. We're going to give him these five guys, and they'll fall in love with them, and we won't have to give up anything until the No. 1 pick a couple years down the line.' That's what they thought."

Herschel Walker (34) was one of the few bright spots for the Cowboys during the 1988 season.

Actually, Walker never did much in Minnesota. Instead of winning Super Bowls, the Vikings ended up with high draft picks that they had to send to Dallas. Using those picks, the Cowboys eventually added running back Emmitt Smith, defensive tackle Russell Maryland, cornerbacks Kevin Smith and Clayton Holmes, and safety Darren Woodson. All of them helped win Super Bowls for the Cowboys.

Johnson wasn't just a trading wizard. He was also quite a coach. By 1991 he'd led the Cowboys to the playoffs for the first time since 1985.

But he also had a quarterback controversy on his hands.

Troy Aikman, who was Jones and Johnson's first-ever draft pick in 1989, had injured his right knee late in the 1991 season. With Aikman on the sidelines, backup Steve Beuerlein stepped in. He played brilliantly, leading the Cowboys to victories in their final five games.

Aikman insisted he was healthy for the wild-card game against the Chicago Bears. He expected to start, but Johnson had other ideas.

Dallas defeated the Bears with Beuerlein under center. Beuerlein then started the second-round game against the Detroit Lions. The Cowboys ended up losing that contest 38–6, with Aikman eventually coming off the bench.

After the game, Aikman thought about seeking a trade. However, Johnson spoke to him a day later and said there would be "no more fooling around" at quarterback. Aikman was his guy.

So were Emmitt Smith and wide receiver Michael Irvin. Together with Aikman, they formed a group known as the Triplets. These three players became the backbone of the Cowboys offense.

MICHAEL IRVIN

Known as "the Playmaker," Michael Irvin was a loud personality. On the field, he let his hands and feet do the talking. And off the field, he was never shy about sharing his opinion.

Irvin had seven seasons with more than 1,000 yards receiving. He made the 1990s All-Decade Team, and he is second on the Cowboys' career receiving list in receptions and yards. During his career, Irvin scored 65 regular-season touchdowns and 8 in the playoffs. He entered the Pro Football Hall of Fame in 2007.

"The thing that gave me an edge was my work ethic," Irvin said. "I was one of those guys who felt, the more you worked, the better you got."

In 1992 Dallas went 13–3 during the regular season, whipped Philadelphia in the playoffs, and then traveled to San Francisco for the NFC Championship Game. The 49ers, who had league MVP Steve Young at quarterback, were favored to win.

No worries. The game ended in a 30–20 Cowboys victory, as Aikman threw for two touchdowns and Smith scored twice. On to the Super Bowl.

"How 'bout them Cowboys?" Johnson shouted.

Michael Irvin (left) celebrates a touchdown with teammate Emmitt Smith during Super Bowl XXVII.

Up next was another postseason regular, the Buffalo Bills, who were making their third straight Super Bowl appearance. The Bills shouldn't have bothered showing up.

In one of the ugliest Super Bowls in history, the Bills committed nine turnovers, two of which the Cowboys returned for touchdowns. It should have been three, but Cowboys defensive tackle Leon Lett showboated on his way to the end zone and was caught from behind. It didn't matter. Dallas crushed Buffalo 52–17.

The Cowboys were NFL champions for the first time since 1977. But Jones and Johnson weren't about to relax. Jones kept spending money on his star players, and Johnson continued to bring in new talent.

The following season, the Cowboys beat San Francisco again for the NFC title. Then they took down Buffalo again to defend their Super Bowl crown. A dynasty was in the making.

Then it blew up.

Jones and Johnson were not getting along, in part because each wanted the most credit for the team's success. In March 1994, they agreed to part ways, with Johnson getting a $2 million payout and becoming an analyst on TV.

Jones would now make all draft picks and trades. He reached out to Barry Switzer, who was once Johnson's archrival at the University of Oklahoma.

Troy Aikman prepares to hand the ball to Smith during the Cowboys' win over the Steelers in Super Bowl XXX.

Switzer agreed to become the new coach of the Cowboys.

Switzer did just fine with Johnson's players, making it to the NFC Championship Game in his first year but losing to the 49ers. In his second year, Switzer guided the Cowboys to their third Super Bowl title in four years with a 27–17 win over the Pittsburgh Steelers.

That victory, which occurred in January 1996, was the last time the Cowboys took home the Lombardi Trophy, as of 2018.

Since 1989, the one constant in the Cowboys organization has been Jones. His powerful role in the NFL earned him a place in the Pro Football Hall of Fame in 2017.

CHAPTER 4

HOME SWEET HOME

The Boston Red Sox have Fenway Park. The Chicago Cubs have Wrigley Field. These historic stadiums have been the longtime homes of two famed sports franchises. The Cowboys have had not just one but three iconic stadiums: the Cotton Bowl, Texas Stadium, and AT&T Stadium. Each place has its role in the history and success of America's Team.

THE COTTON BOWL

Originally built in the 1930s for Southern Methodist University's football team, the Cotton Bowl is located a couple miles east of downtown Dallas. The stadium cost $328,000 to construct–which might not sound

Attendance at the Cotton Bowl was sparse during a 1960 game between the Cowboys and Browns.

like a lot, but that's more than $4 million in today's dollars. And America was going through the Great Depression at the time.

The stadium originally held 45,000 people. However, the capacity reached 92,000 by 2008.

Though the Cotton Bowl was SMU's home field, the stadium's biggest game has always been the Red River Rivalry. Held during the State Fair of Texas, this annual contest pits the University of Texas against the University of Oklahoma. For that game in early October, the stands are filled with the orange colors of the Texas Longhorns and the red of the Oklahoma Sooners.

But what about Cowboys blue?

When the Cowboys were born in 1960, they had to share the Cotton Bowl with the Dallas Texans. The Texans, also founded in 1960, were a member of the American Football League (AFL), which was competing with the NFL in those days. The Texans spent three seasons in Big D, won the AFL title in 1962, and then moved to Kansas City–in part because they couldn't compete with the Cowboys.

For one thing, the NFL had bigger stars. When the likes of Jim Brown or Johnny Unitas came to town to play the Cowboys, fans flocked to the Cotton Bowl.

Cowboys quarterback Don Meredith hands the ball to Don Perkins during the 1966 NFL Championship Game at the Cotton Bowl.

Before long, though, the Cowboys themselves were the main attraction. The team went 7–7 in 1965, which was their first year without a losing record.

In 1966 Dallas won the Eastern Division and hosted the Green Bay Packers—the league's dynasty of that era—for the NFL Championship Game. On New Year's Day 1967, the first NFL title game played in Texas was a thriller. In fact, it was one of the greatest matches in Cotton Bowl stadium history.

"Nothing could compare with this," said Mark Duncan, supervisor of officials for the NFL at the time. "This game had everything: tremendous execution by both offenses against two of the best defenses in football; a fast start by the Packers; a great rally by a young team like the Cowboys; and then, of course, that finish."

That finish capped a wild affair in which Green Bay scored two early touchdowns only to see the Cowboys tie it 14–14 before the end of the first quarter. The Packers led 21–20 in the third period, and they scored two more touchdowns to make it 34–20.

The Cotton Bowl was quiet.

Rather than accept that the more-experienced Packers were the better team, the Cowboys got the fans cheering again with a 68-yard touchdown pass from Don Meredith to Frank Clarke. Then the Cowboys got the ball back and began marching toward Green Bay's end zone. Soon, Dallas was at the Packers' 2-yard line in the game's final minute. Fourth down. Could the Cowboys score a touchdown to force overtime?

Meredith rolled right, looking to run or throw. Packers linebacker Dave Robinson broke through and grabbed Meredith in the backfield. Meredith somehow

DON MEREDITH

Don Meredith was a good quarterback during his nine seasons with Dallas, but he became far more famous after retiring. In 1970 he joined the new *Monday Night Football* broadcast as an analyst.

Nicknamed "Dandy Don," Meredith was known as much for his joking around in the broadcast booth as for how he broke down plays. He was the exact opposite of the other analyst, the always-serious Howard Cosell. Both were over-the-top announcers in different ways, and their popularity soared.

During his playing career, Meredith went 47–32–4 as a starter for the Cowboys. He entered the team's Ring of Honor in 1976.

tossed a weak sidearm throw into the end zone. But Packers safety Tom Brown intercepted it, sealing Green Bay's 34–27 victory.

The most memorable NFL game in the Cotton Bowl ended in disappointment for the Cowboys.

By the next year, team owner Clint Murchison Jr. wanted a new stadium. He believed the Cotton Bowl was too old, had uncomfortable seats, and wasn't big enough. It was time to move.

TEXAS STADIUM

When Texas Stadium opened in 1971, some fans wondered if the Cowboys had forgotten something. After all, there was a big hole in the roof. Cowboys linebacker D. D. Lewis offered an explanation for why the hole was there.

"So God can watch his favorite team play," he said.

Texas Stadium was located in Irving, a suburb of Dallas. The new stadium had all the upgrades Murchison wished for. The $35 million building included 381 luxury boxes, special club areas, and more than 64,000 comfortable seats. And most of the seats were shaded, despite the hole in the roof.

The idea for the hole came from European soccer stadiums, many of which had a similar design. There was just one problem: while fans in the stands remained dry, the field was at the mercy of Mother Nature. Never was that more obvious than on Thanksgiving Day 1993.

The Dallas area was hit with a blizzard. That might not be a problem in Green Bay or Buffalo, but snow is a foreign object in Big D. The field was a mess, with wind blowing the white stuff everywhere. But at least the home crowd was about to see their Cowboys defeat the Miami Dolphins. Or so it seemed.

The Cowboys huddle on a snow-covered field during a 1993 Thanksgiving Day game against the Dolphins.

Enter Leon Lett.

Dallas led 14–13 in the game's closing moments, and a Cowboys victory appeared certain. The Dolphins' quarterback, future Hall of Famer Dan Marino, was out with a torn Achilles tendon. Even so, backup quarterback Steve DeBerg got the Dolphins in position for a 41-yard field goal attempt. It was hardly an easy kick in the near-whiteout.

Dallas defenders surged through the line and blocked the kick. As the ball skittered harmlessly toward the Cowboys' goal line, the frozen fans began celebrating. Then Lett, a Cowboys defensive tackle, tried to fall on the ball. What a mistake. If nobody had touched the ball, the Cowboys would have gained possession when it stopped rolling. But for some reason, Lett went for it. He couldn't handle the slippery pigskin, though, and the Dolphins recovered.

After much confusion–there was no replay review at the time–the referee awarded possession to Miami. Dolphins kicker Pete Stoyanovich nailed a much simpler 19-yarder for the victory.

"I knew the rule," Lett said years later. "I had blocked field goals in the past. It's not like it was my first time on the field goal block team. Maybe it was that season, but not in my career. I have been trying to think back for, what, 20 years now, and I don't know what happened. It was a brain freeze."

Despite the tough loss to the Dolphins, Texas Stadium saw far more Cowboys wins than losses. In fact, Dallas went 213–100 during its 37 years in the building. All five of the Cowboys' Super Bowl teams played at Texas Stadium, and flags celebrating each championship hung from the ceiling.

After the final game there, nearly 100 former players and 12 members of the Ring of Honor paid tribute to the stadium.

Leon Lett makes an ill-advised attempt to grab the ball after a blocked field goal.

AT&T STADIUM

Jerry Jones loves to talk about what inspired him to build a new stadium for the Cowboys. The story begins in the mid-1960s when Jones was a member of the Arkansas Razorbacks football team.

"I was a senior in college," Jones said. "Our coach took us to Houston . . . on a field trip to the Astrodome, the eighth wonder of the world. There had never yet been a game played in it."

When Jones entered the world's first domed stadium, he was amazed.

"It was like Mars," he said. "Where do you start to build something like this, where do you hit the first nail or turn the first screw?"

> "It was like Mars. . . . Where do you start to build something like this, where do you hit the first nail or turn the first screw?"
>
> —Jerry Jones on seeing the Astrodome for the first time

Three decades later, Jones had similar questions when he began thinking about a new stadium for the Cowboys.

"How do you pay for it, make it work, get our leaders to be part of it?" he asked himself. "But I didn't have to wonder if I could do it. I knew I could do it. I'd seen it done. And you could put five of those stadiums into our stadium."

AT&T Stadium—originally called Cowboys Stadium and affectionately known as Jerry World—is monstrous in size. It seats 80,000 people for football and as many as 100,000 for special events. The stadium is located in Arlington, which is between Dallas and Fort Worth.

And on a clear day, the stadium can be seen from both cities. Fly into the local airport and it's impossible not to notice.

It's also hard not to notice that the Cowboys haven't fared so well there. Heading into the 2018 season, they were 37–35 at Jerry World. At one point, they lost eight home games in a row.

Head coach Jason Garrett didn't make excuses. "My response is we just need to focus on coaching better and playing better, regardless of where we play–our stadium, someone else's stadium, in the parking lot, and on the moon," he said. "Hopefully that will lead to the outcomes we want."

Regardless of those outcomes, the fans keep coming. And why not: the place is awesome. It cost just over $1 billion to build, making it 30 times more expensive than Texas Stadium. Jones paid more than half of the bill himself. Meanwhile, the city of Arlington was willing to spend enough ($325 million) to get the Cowboys to move there.

AT&T Stadium's main entrance features a glass wall that stands an impressive 800 feet tall. Inside, there's a retractable glass door at each end zone. Measuring 180 feet wide by 120 feet high, they are among the largest glass doors in the world. The stadium also has a

Cowboys fans packed the stands during the first game at the new stadium in 2009.

retractable roof (no hole this time), wider seats than most stadiums, 15,000 club seats, and 200 suites.

Until the Atlanta Falcons opened their new building in 2017, AT&T Stadium had the largest video board in

an American stadium. It hangs above the center of the field, with four screens stretching 50 yards.

Whether the home team is winning or not, AT&T Stadium is a must-see.

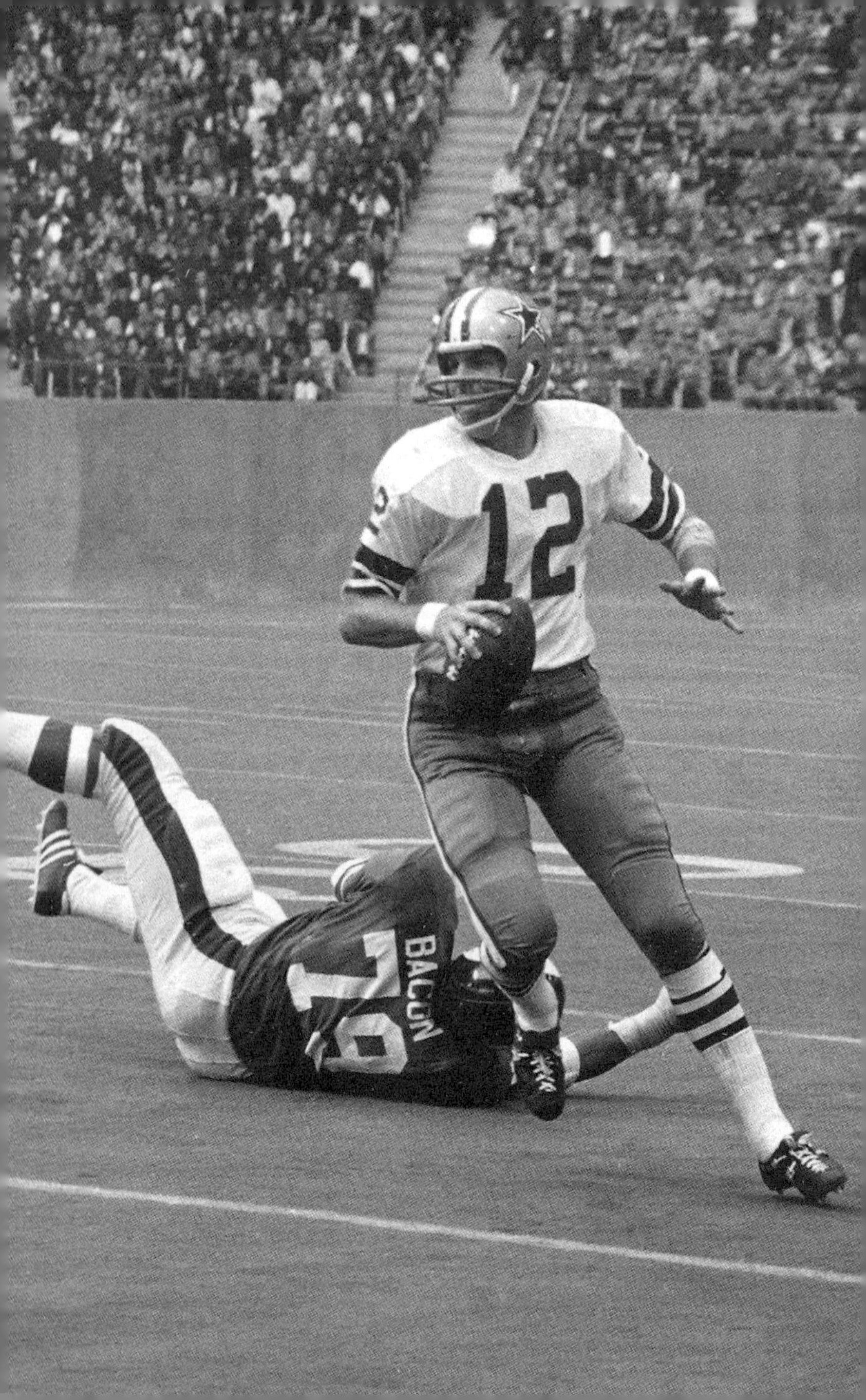
12
BACON

CHAPTER 5

ROGER, TROY, AND TONY

Some franchises are measured by their running backs or defenses. Others are measured by their coaches. While Dallas has had greatness in all of those areas, the team's quarterbacks stand out the most. The three best quarterbacks in Cowboys history are Roger Staubach, Troy Aikman, and Tony Romo.

ROGER

Very few stories are as inspirational as Staubach's. Born and raised in Ohio, he decided to play quarterback for the Naval Academy, which in the early 1960s was a football power. Staubach won the 1963 Heisman

Roger Staubach eludes a defender, showing how he earned the nickname "Roger the Dodger."

Trophy as college football's top player and was an All-American.

Students who attend military academies make a commitment to serve after graduating. For this reason, few athletes from the academies even attempt to turn pro in their sport. Staubach's journey began like most of his classmates. After the '64 season, he began four years of military service, which included a tour in Vietnam. But Staubach was determined to pursue pro football. And the Cowboys remained interested.

So in 1969, as a 27-year-old rookie, Staubach climbed aboard the Dallas ship.

He didn't become the starter until replacing a struggling Craig Morton during a loss to Chicago in 1971. Staubach led Dallas to wins in all seven remaining games. Then in the playoffs, he led his team past Minnesota and San Francisco to get the Cowboys back to the Super Bowl. They'd lost the previous year to the Colts. But this time Staubach, helped by running back Duane Thomas and the Doomsday Defense, took home the Lombardi Trophy.

Dallas was almost a regular visitor to the Super Bowl with Staubach, going four times and winning twice. Ironically, the second victory was against the

Staubach attempts a pass during Super Bowl X against the Pittsburgh Steelers.

Denver Broncos in January 1978. They were led by Morton–the man Staubach had replaced.

Opposing players had plenty of good things to say about Staubach.

> "He is one of the finest to ever play the game. . . . I think if I had some of that Staubach competitiveness, I'd have been much better."
>
> –Packers quarterback Bart Starr

"He is one of the finest to ever play the game," said fellow Hall of Fame quarterback Bart Starr. "I think if I had some of that Staubach competitiveness, I'd have been much better."

Staubach had no shortage of nicknames. He was known as Roger the Dodger for his footwork, Captain America for his service to the country, and Captain Comeback for never panicking when Dallas fell behind.

"You could never defeat Roger mentally or physically," Cowboys coach Tom Landry said in 1983.

TROY

Troy Aikman began his college career at the University of Oklahoma. While there, he played for coach Barry Switzer, who would later lead Aikman and the Cowboys to a Super Bowl championship.

But Aikman wasn't getting as much playing time as he wanted in Oklahoma, so he transferred to the University of California, Los Angeles. That's where he became a star passer.

When Jerry Jones bought the Cowboys in 1989, he and new coach Jimmy Johnson made Aikman their first draft selection. In fact, they chose Aikman with the first pick in the entire 1989 draft. However, Dallas promptly went 1–15, and Aikman started in 11 of those losses.

But the Cowboys knew if they built a team around Aikman, he would become a star. In 1992 he did exactly that. Aikman guided Dallas to the NFC East crown and then into the Super Bowl.

Against Buffalo, Aikman was unstoppable. He threw for four touchdowns in a 52–17 laugher.

The Cowboys repeated as champions in the 1993 season, and Aikman had an even better season. He topped the NFL by completing 69.1 percent of his passes.

Although Dallas fell short of the Super Bowl after the 1994 season, losing in the NFC title game to San Francisco, Aikman and the team rebounded the next year with yet another championship. That gave him

Troy Aikman prepares to fire a pass during a 1993 win over Washington.

three Super Bowl wins in four seasons—a record that has been matched but not broken.

Aikman's 90 wins in the 1990s set an NFL record for a single decade. When he retired in 2001, he held 47 Cowboys passing records. And five years later, Aikman became a Hall of Famer.

"In my mind, I always judge a quarterback by how he plays in the big games," said Johnson, who coached

Aikman to two championships. "How does he perform in the playoffs? Troy Aikman always came up big in the big games."

TONY

Unlike Aikman, who was the top pick in the NFL Draft, Tony Romo was ignored. Romo was a fine college quarterback. But he played for Eastern Illinois, a second-tier school not known for producing pro players.

The Cowboys had low expectations for Romo when they signed him as an undrafted free agent in 2003. Romo served as a backup to veterans Quincy Carter, Vinny Testaverde, and Drew Bledsoe before getting his chance in 2006. After that, he never looked back. By the time he retired, Romo had set team records for passing yards and touchdown passes.

For all his regular-season magic, Romo struggled in the playoffs. Perhaps his most memorable (or forgettable) moment was a January 2007 playoff game against the Seattle Seahawks. With less than two minutes left, Romo was the holder for a short field goal attempt that would have given Dallas the lead. But he fumbled the snap. The kick never got off, and the Seahawks held on for the victory.

During his career, Romo went 78–49 as an injury-prone starter. Those injuries finally caught up to him in 2016. When Romo hurt his back in the preseason, rookie quarterback Dak Prescott stepped in—and he played phenomenally, eventually winning the Offensive Rookie of the Year Award.

There was a new star in Dallas, and Romo knew his time was up. Still, Romo was one of the most popular Cowboys for a decade.

Tony Romo looks for a receiver during a 2014 game in Philadelphia.

"He makes his teammates better," said coach Jason Garrett. "He makes his coaches better. He makes his team better. . . . It has been one of the great privileges of my life to work with Tony Romo, one of the greatest players in Dallas Cowboys history."

CHAPTER 6

ERA OF DISAPPOINTMENT

For all the Cowboys' dominance in the 1970s and 1990s, the last quarter-century has not been kind to America's Team. Sure, they won their division a handful of times in that span, and they had a few wild-card berths along the way. But they also had three consecutive 5–11 seasons and three straight 8–8 seasons.

Unlike those glory years when Tom Landry and Jimmy Johnson were the head coaches, the Cowboys have gone through several since Barry Switzer led the team to the 1995 crown. And going into the 2018

Tony Romo's botched hold on a field goal attempt became a symbol of the Cowboys' struggles in the 2000s.

season, Dallas hadn't been back to the Super Bowl since.

"I would have bet I'll be back," owner Jerry Jones said in 2016 when asked about the championship drought. "When I look back at it, I think I might have (felt) entitled to Super Bowls. You can get that feeling coming out of that. Maybe this is your special spotlight here. You're going to be able to rack up five, six, seven, eight of these."

But over time, Jones began to realize he was overconfident.

"Well, the good old reality hard light of the day hit, and I do appreciate and respect just how difficult this thing is."

It's not as if the Cowboys haven't had good players. Even though they went 3–8 in playoff games between 1996 and 2017, they've had plenty of stars wearing the star.

Quarterback is always a key to success. After Troy Aikman retired in 2001, the Cowboys went through eight starters until Tony Romo emerged in 2006. Though Romo struggled in the playoffs, he smashed Aikman's team records for regular-season touchdowns and passing yards.

DALLAS COWBOYS CHEERLEADERS

One area in which the Cowboys always lead the league is cheerleading. The Dallas Cowboys Cheerleaders, established in 1972, are known throughout America. The cheerleading team, which is featured on its own TV show, is famous for its precise dancing and iconic uniforms. In fact, when the Cowboys played in London, England, in 2014, the cheerleaders were as popular as the players.

"Who you are really matters," said Emma Mary, who was in her fourth year as a cheerleader for that England trip. "We truly are America's sweethearts. We're representing the Dallas Cowboys wherever we go whether it's at our job, at our church, or in London. We don't have an offseason. Maybe two weeks in January–unless we get booked. We're constantly performing, but we love it that way."

After depending on Emmitt Smith during the glory years, the Cowboys didn't have another star running back until DeMarco Murray led the league in rushing in 2014.

Wide receiver Michael Irvin was another key to the Cowboys' success in the 1990s. Since then, the team has had other star receivers. For instance, Terrell

Jason Witten played all 15 seasons of his incredible career with the Dallas Cowboys.

Owens had three solid seasons between 2006 and 2008. But Owens was known as a difficult teammate, and the Cowboys eventually let him go. Dez Bryant was an outstanding receiver for most of his eight seasons in Dallas, but the team cut him in 2018.

Until Dallas began using high draft picks on offensive linemen–tackle Tyron Smith in 2011, center Travis Frederick in 2013, and guard Zack Martin in 2014–the blocking had been poor for much of the 2000s. The only constant was tight end Jason Witten. From 2003 to 2017, he had 1,152 catches (fourth-most in NFL history) along with 68 touchdowns.

> “Every practice, every film session, every notebook I filled, every ounce of sweat, I did so because of my love and drive for the game of football.”
>
> –Jason Witten

“For the past 15 years, every practice, every film session, every notebook I filled, every ounce of sweat, I did so because of my love and drive for the game of football,” Witten said when he retired. “And I tried my absolute best to be dependable–dependable to my teammates, to my coaches, to my family and to all those who were cheering us on." Fans haven't had much to cheer for on defense since the late 1990s. Dallas ranked 20th or worse in points allowed eight times. But that doesn't mean the Cowboys were without defensive stars. Leading the way were linebackers DeMarcus Ware and Sean Lee, defensive backs Darren Woodson and Terence Newman, and defensive linemen La'Roi Glover and Greg Ellis. Sure, there were some good players. There simply weren't enough good plays.

Despite the lack of championships in recent years, the Cowboys have still received plenty of attention since their last Super Bowl win. That was certainly true in the late 2010s, when Dallas had a dominating running back in Ezekiel Elliott, a promising young quarterback in Dak Prescott, and one of the best offensive lines in the NFL. And when Dallas hosted the 2018 NFL Draft, there was yet another shining spotlight on the Cowboys.

Turns out America's Team is hard to ignore.

Dak Prescott launches a pass during a 2017 win over the Eagles.

CHAPTER 7

CLASSIC GAMES

The Hail Mary win at Minnesota wasn't the first classic game that the Cowboys were involved in, and it wasn't the last. Here are some of the other great games the team has played—including a few tough losses.

NFL CHAMPIONSHIP GAME ("THE ICE BOWL")—DECEMBER 31, 1967

The temperature at game time was 13 degrees below zero. The wind chill was a mind-numbing 40 below. Much of the Lambeau Field turf was frozen. Yet 50,000 Green Bay Packers fans crowded into the stadium. When the referee blew his whistle to start the game, it froze to his lips.

This type of weather was unheard of in Dallas. So it was little surprise when Green Bay took a 14–0 lead

Cowboys defensive end George Andrie picks up a Packers fumble during the Ice Bowl.

in the second quarter. The Cowboys, not accustomed to such cold, would have been forgiven for throwing in the towel. Instead, they scored 17 straight points—including a halfback pass by Dan Reeves for the go-ahead score early in the fourth quarter.

But the Packers weren't done. On the final drive of the game, they marched down the field. With only 16 seconds remaining, Green Bay had the ball inside the Cowboys' 1-yard line. Packers coach Vince Lombardi decided not to attempt a game-tying field goal. No one wanted to stay out there for overtime, anyway.

Instead, Packers quarterback Bart Starr plunged into the end zone on a sneak to win the game. It was the bitterest (and coldest) of endings for Dallas.

SUPER BOWL V—JANUARY 17, 1971

The Cowboys' first Super Bowl appearance was also their sloppiest. They committed four turnovers against the Baltimore Colts, including a late interception with the score tied at 13. The Colts were even sloppier, with an incredible seven turnovers. Still, Baltimore managed to win the game thanks to a 32-yard field goal from Jim O'Brien with just five seconds remaining.

SUPER BOWL VI—JANUARY 16, 1972

It wasn't just redemption. It was one of the easiest Super Bowl wins ever.

The Miami Dolphins never really challenged Dallas in Super Bowl VI. Early in the first quarter, the Cowboys' famous Doomsday Defense forced a fumble by Larry Csonka, who almost never fumbled. After that, it was all downhill for the Dolphins. Miami gained only 185 yards in the game, compared with 352 for Dallas. The game ended in a 24–3 romp that gave the Cowboys their first Super Bowl championship.

NFC DIVISIONAL PLAYOFF—DECEMBER 23, 1972

This game is perhaps the ultimate example of why Roger Staubach was known as Captain Comeback. Down to the 49ers 28–13 in the fourth quarter, Cowboys coach Tom Landry replaced Craig Morton with Staubach, who had been sidelined by a shoulder injury. Staubach then threw for two touchdowns in the final minutes for a 30–28 victory.

"I think the biggest thing about Roger is that he never quit," Cowboys defensive tackle Bob Lilly said. "It didn't matter how much the Cowboys were down."

SUPER BOWL X—JANUARY 18, 1976

In the 1970s, hardly anyone could challenge the Pittsburgh Steelers and their dreaded Steel Curtain defense. The Cowboys tried, even leading 10–7 at halftime. But a blocked punt for a safety jump-started a Steelers comeback. Pittsburgh quarterback Terry Bradshaw later connected with Lynn Swann on a 64-yard touchdown pass that turned out to be the difference maker. It was another Super Bowl disappointment for the Cowboys.

SUPER BOWL XII—JANUARY 15, 1978

Dallas crushed the Orange Crush. The Denver Broncos, led by former Cowboys quarterback Craig Morton, were the surprise winners of the AFC and appearing in their first Super Bowl. But Morton was no match for his former backup, Roger Staubach—or for the Doomsdayers, who intercepted Morton four times.

The Cowboys defense had four sacks and allowed only eight completed passes in a 27–10 win.

SUPER BOWL XIII—JANUARY 21, 1979

This one was a rematch of 1976. And this time the Steelers, in addition to their tough defense, had some offensive firepower. Still, if Cowboys tight end Jackie

Cowboys defensive end Ed "Too Tall" Jones crushes Broncos quarterback Craig Morton during Super Bowl XII.

Smith hadn't dropped a pass in the end zone, Dallas might have defended its crown.

In a wild shootout that some consider the best Super Bowl ever, Bradshaw threw for four touchdowns and Staubach for three. At one point the Cowboys trailed 35–17, but Captain Comeback brought them to within four. However, the Steelers couldn't be denied, and they held on for the victory.

NFC CHAMPIONSHIP GAME—JANUARY 10, 1982

Don't ever mention "the Catch" around Cowboys fans. Sure, it's one of the most famous plays in NFL history—but it's one of the most painful for Dallas.

With San Francisco trailing 27–21 and the clock ticking toward zero, 49ers quarterback Joe Montana took his team downfield. From the Dallas 6-yard line, Montana rolled right as Cowboys defenders chased him. Just before stepping out of bounds, Montana sent a high pass into the back corner of the end zone. Wide receiver Dwight Clark, running from the other side of the end zone, leaped into the air and made a fingertip catch. The extra point lifted San Francisco to victory and paved the way for the team's dynasty of the 1980s.

SUPER BOWL XXVII—JANUARY 31, 1993

"How 'bout them Cowboys?"

That was coach Jimmy Johnson's reaction whenever his team did something special. And Super Bowl XXVII, a 52–17 rout of Buffalo, was special indeed. Troy Aikman threw for four touchdowns, and the defense ran two fumbles into the end zone. The victory marked the Cowboys' first NFL championship since the 1977 season.

COWBOYS AT GIANTS—JANUARY 2, 1994

Dallas faced the New York Giants in the final game of the 1993 regular season. Both teams were 11–4 going into the contest, and the winner would clinch home-field advantage throughout the playoffs. The loser would make the playoffs as a wild-card team.

Things looked grim for the Cowboys when running back Emmitt Smith separated his shoulder in the first half. But he played the rest of the game and basically beat the Giants one-handed. Smith ran for 168 yards and caught 10 passes for another 61 yards.

In an overtime thriller, Dallas came out on top. It was perhaps the greatest regular-season game in Cowboys history.

SUPER BOWL XXVIII—JANUARY 30, 1994

In a rematch against Buffalo, the Cowboys had to try a bit harder than last time. The Bills established a 13–6 lead by halftime, and it looked like Buffalo might finally win its first Super Bowl. But early in the third quarter, Dallas safety James Washington recovered a fumble and went 48 yards for a game-tying touchdown.

Buffalo never recovered. Emmitt Smith, who rushed for 132 yards and two touchdowns, was voted Super Bowl MVP. Jimmy Johnson's last game as Cowboys coach saw him carried off the field on players' shoulders.

SUPER BOWL XXX—JANUARY 28, 1996

This time with Barry Switzer as coach, Dallas became the first team to win three Super Bowls in four years. Cornerback Larry Brown had two huge interceptions, Smith scored twice, and the Cowboys finally beat the Steelers in a title game.

NFC DIVISIONAL PLAYOFF—JANUARY 11, 2015

Known as the "No-Catch Game," Cowboys fans will always believe their team was robbed.

Trailing the Packers 26–21, Dallas moved downfield in the game's final minutes. On fourth and two from

Dez Bryant makes a spectacular catch against the Packers in the closing minutes of a playoff game, but officials later reversed the call.

Green Bay's 32-yard line, Tony Romo threw a perfect pass to a diving Dez Bryant. Making an amazing grab, Bryant caught the ball at the 1-yard line.

Just one problem.

As Bryant hit the ground, the ball moved a few inches while in his hands. After a video review, officials overturned the call. The Packers took over possession and held on to win the game.

Three years later, the NFL changed its catch rule. Under the new rule, Bryant's "no-catch" would have been a completion.

CHAPTER 8

GREAT RIVALRIES

When you're known as America's Team, everyone is a rival. Not only do the Dallas Cowboys recognize that—they like it. They also like the fact that hundreds, if not thousands, of Cowboys fans fill the stands when they visit any stadium in the country. Sometimes, especially in places where the local team doesn't sell out games, there are more folks rooting for Dallas than there are cheering on the home team.

In fact, a 2017 study showed that 10 percent of all people who follow the NFL considered themselves Cowboys fans.

Yep, Cowboys fans are everywhere. When owner Jerry Jones was inducted into the Pro Football Hall of Fame in 2017, the stadium in Canton, Ohio, was

A scuffle breaks out between two bitter rivals after the Cowboys score a touchdown against the Redskins in 2013.

Cowboys defenders rough up legendary Packers quarterback Brett Favre (4) during a playoff game in January 1995.

packed—with his team's faithful, and with the entire Cowboys roster of players and coaches.

"I leave you tonight with one last thank you," Jones said in his speech. "It's for you, the fans. I'm a fan. You're the heartbeat of the game. And the Dallas Cowboy fans are the greatest fans on earth. But I love Giant fans. I love Eagle fans. I love Redskin fans. I love Massillon High School fans here. I love McKinley fans right here in town. You're here tonight because you love the game. Guys, I'm here because I love it, too."

Of course, not everyone likes the Cowboys. That's especially true of the three opponents in the NFC East, whom Dallas faces twice a season: the New York Giants, Philadelphia Eagles, and Washington Redskins. It's also true of two franchises the Cowboys don't play every year, but which have been great rivals through the decades–especially in the playoffs.

Here's a look at those rivalries.

GREEN BAY PACKERS

Heading into the 2018 season, the Packers led the all-time series 19–17. Eight of those matchups came in the playoffs, with each team winning four. That includes the league championships in 1966 and 1967, which Green Bay won to earn a trip to the first two Super Bowls.

Dallas had its glory days against the Pack in the 1990s, winning three straight postseason games. At one point in that decade, when the Cowboys had the Triplets, they beat Green Bay eight straight times.

But the Packers had a string of five victories in a row from 2009 to 2015 with Aaron Rodgers at quarterback.

"Ahhh, yeah," said Packers receiver Jordy Nelson, who was Rodgers' favorite target during many of those Green Bay wins. "It's a good conversation, for the fans. There's a lot of history there in the past, and I think we've had a lot of history just recently, too. . . . And so it's just some big games; big games and some incredible finishes."

When Rodgers, Nelson, and the Packers reached the Super Bowl after the 2010 season, the game was played in Cowboys Stadium. Watching the cheeseheads celebrate a championship on Cowboys turf had to be painful for Dallas fans.

PITTSBURGH STEELERS

How could teams from two different conferences create a bitter rivalry?

By playing in some epic Super Bowls.

Heading into the 2018 season, Dallas led the all-time series 17–15. The teams have met in three Super Bowls. Pittsburgh came out on top in the 1975 and 1978 seasons, and Dallas took home the title in the 1995 season.

Both teams were dominators in the 1970s. Dallas won two NFL championships while Pittsburgh, led by the Steel Curtain defense, won four.

Cowboys linebacker Lee Roy Jordan takes down Steelers running back Franco Harris during Super Bowl X.

Great teams loaded with great players make for such awesome rivalries. Consider that 15 Hall of Famers played in the two Super Bowls in the 1970s: ten from Pittsburgh, five from Dallas. Both coaches, Chuck Noll and Tom Landry, are also in the Hall.

"It's one of the great rivalries in all of sports, and it's been like that long before I showed up here," said Cowboys coach Jason Garrett, who took charge midway through the 2010 season. "They played against each other in the '70s: two marquee franchises that were winning the Super Bowl."

NEW YORK GIANTS

If it seems like the TV networks love this rivalry . . . well, they do.

Since 2009, when AT&T Stadium opened, the Cowboys and Giants have played in numerous nationally televised games. Dallas has won plenty of them, but the one that hurt was the first-ever game at Jerry World.

A record crowd of 105,121 filled the stands, and there was no shortage of celebrities. Former President George W. Bush and First Lady Laura Bush did the coin toss. Basketball star LeBron James was in the crowd. And the new Ring of Honor was unveiled during a halftime ceremony featuring Roger Staubach, Bob Lilly, Troy Aikman, Emmitt Smith, and Michael Irvin.

Oh yes, there was a game, too. Unfortunately for Cowboys fans, it featured a superb performance by Giants quarterback Eli Manning. He threw for 330 yards and two touchdown passes, bringing New York from behind four times. Manning led two fourth-quarter drives that resulted in field goals by

Giants defensive end Mathias Kiwanuka and Cowboys tackle Flozell Adams show that there's no love lost between these two teams.

Lawrence Tynes. The second of those was a 37-yarder to win the game with no time remaining.

After the Giants victory, Manning wrote his name on a wall near the visiting locker room. He added a message that was sure to annoy Cowboys fans: "'33-31' First win in the new stadium."

There's no denying that the loss stung. Overall, though, Dallas has had the upper hand in the rivalry. Entering the 2018 season, the Cowboys led the series 64–46–2.

The first meeting was back in 1960 at the old Yankee Stadium in New York. The Giants had a respectable 5–3–1 record going into the game, while the Cowboys were 0–10.

Cowboys coach Tom Landry had been the Giants' defensive coordinator from 1954 to 1959. But New York's owner, Wellington Mara, suggested that the Cowboys hire Landry as their head man when they debuted in 1960. That's exactly what the Cowboys did.

Landry repaid Mara by leading Dallas to a 31–31 tie against the Giants. At first the Cowboys appeared headed for yet another loss, but quarterback Eddie LeBron threw two touchdown passes in the final quarter. It was the Cowboys' only non-defeat in 1960.

From there, things got much better for Dallas—except in the postseason. The only playoff meeting between the two teams occurred after the 2007 season. The Giants won 21–17 at Texas Stadium and went on to claim the Super Bowl crown.

But the one game that Cowboys fans will always remember was Emmitt Smith's unbelievable performance in the final week of the 1993 regular season. Even with a separated shoulder, Smith practically won the game single-handedly.

PHILADELPHIA EAGLES

Philadelphia is known as the City of Brotherly Love. But that doesn't apply to the Cowboys.

Heading into the 2018 season, the Cowboys led the series 66–52, including a record of 3–1 in the playoffs. Games between the Cowboys and Eagles tend to be rough, ugly, and sometimes dirty. After all, this is the rivalry that ended Michael Irvin's career with a back injury in 1999. Eagles fans actually cheered when Irvin went down and lay motionless on the turf. And they cheered again when he was wheeled off on a stretcher.

Irvin claimed those cheers were out of respect. Eagles fans would probably disagree.

"It was a compliment for Philly to cheer me," said Irvin. "Philly wasn't cheering my injury. They were cheering my departure: 'Thank God he's leaving the field, he's been killing us. Thank God, maybe now we have a chance to win.'"

An official tries to break up a skirmish between Eagles cornerback Nolan Carroll and Cowboys wide receiver Dwayne Harris.

Given the bad blood between the two teams, any Dallas win against Philadelphia is big. But two of the biggest came in the playoffs after the 1992 and 1995 seasons. The first was a 34–10 triumph that marked the first home playoff win for Jimmy Johnson's crew led by the Triplets. Dallas outgained Philly 346 yards to 178 and had five sacks. The second meeting was just as lopsided. Eagles quarterback Randall Cunningham, one of the better scrambling quarterbacks in NFL history, went down four times. Dallas cruised to a

30–11 victory. And sweetest of all, the Cowboys went on to win the Super Bowl both of those years.

WASHINGTON REDSKINS

Of all the Cowboys' rivalries—and there are many—this is probably the most intense. It dates back to before the Cowboys even existed.

In the late 1950s, Clint Murchison Jr. was trying to start an NFL franchise in Dallas. However, Washington owner George Preston Marshall tried to block the deal. He feared a team in Dallas would shrink the Redskins' fan base. But Murchison had bought the rights to "Hail to the Redskins," a song played at every Redskins home game. That meant Marshall needed Murchison's permission to use the song. So Marshall voted for expansion to Dallas, and Murchison gave back the rights to the song.

But the off-field stuff doesn't end there. Not even close.

George Allen, the Redskins' coach from 1971 to 1977, used to tell his team he would fight Cowboys coach Tom Landry to win a game.

Redskins defensive tackle Diron Talbert once refused to shake Roger Staubach's hand during the coin toss. He claimed he was joking, but the Hall of

Dallas defenders sack Washington quarterback Joe Theismann during a game in January 1983.

Fame quarterback took it seriously enough to ask Talbert at a postseason dinner why he hated him so much.

Cowboys defensive end Harvey Martin once received a funeral wreath with a card reading "From the Redskins." He tossed it inside the Washington locker room, but Landry made him apologize.

And then there's the on-field stuff.

In 1984 Redskins quarterback Joe Theismann ran around with a late snap rather than take a knee. On the next snap, cornerback Ron Fellows dived over the linemen to get at Theismann. Punches flew.

The classic Cowboys–Redskins game occurred on Thanksgiving Day 1974. Well, at least from the Dallas side it was a classic.

The Cowboys had a 6–5 record going into the game, and they trailed Washington by two games in the NFC East. Talbert had said the best way to beat Dallas that day would be to knock out Cowboys quarterback Roger Staubach. And the Redskins did exactly that. Staubach left with a concussion in the third quarter.

Enter rookie quarterback Clint Longley, best known for his hobby of rattlesnake hunting. He hadn't taken a snap all season.

Washington led 16–3, but Longley connected with tight end Billy Joe Dupree for a 35-yard score. Not long after, Longley guided a 70-yard drive that ended in a 1-yard touchdown run by Walt Garrison. Dallas had taken a 17–16 lead.

"He was unbelievable for a guy who hasn't played," Garrison said after the game. "One time I brought in a play and started to explain things to him and he said, 'Shut up, Walt!'"

The Redskins rallied to go ahead 23–17. They seemed ready for more, but Cowboys defensive star Ed "Too Tall" Jones blocked a field goal.

Still, it looked like a rotten Thanksgiving for Big D when Drew Pearson fumbled in the fourth quarter. But the Cowboys forced a punt, and Longley would get one more chance with 1:45 left.

On fourth down, he completed a 6-yard pass at midfield to Bob Hayes. Then, with only 35 seconds remaining, Longley dropped back and launched a deep pass into double coverage. Pearson ran through both defenders, caught the ball in stride, and galloped into the end zone.

"The Mad Bomber" had won the game.

TALE OF THE TAPE

COWBOYS VS. REDSKINS

	COWBOYS	REDSKINS
All-time record	502-374-6 (.573)	593-581-28 (.506)
Head-to-head record (including playoffs)	70-44-2	44-70-2
Super Bowl record	5-3	3-2
NFL championships (pre-1966)	0	2
Hall of Famers	16	20

** Accurate through the 2017 season.*

74

CHAPTER 9

MOUNT RUSHMORE

Deciding on just four players for the Dallas Cowboys' Mount Rushmore is challenging. Almost as challenging as blocking Bob Lilly, sacking Roger Staubach, or tackling Tony Dorsett and Emmitt Smith.

You could make a convincing argument for several other Dallas greats—and that's a good problem to have if you're a Cowboys fan. But in the end, there can only be four.

BOB LILLY (1961–1974)

Maybe all you need to know about defensive lineman Bob Lilly is his nickname: Mr. Cowboy. Lilly was the first draft pick by the franchise in 1961. He was born

Bob Lilly made a career of throwing opponents around like rag dolls.

in Olney, Texas, just a couple hours outside Dallas. He went to Texas Christian University, where he made the All-American team. Then he played his entire 14-year pro career with the Cowboys.

Lilly burst onto the NFL scene, winning Rookie of the Year honors even though Dallas went 4–9–1. From there, Lilly made seven All-Pro teams. He was chosen for 11 Pro Bowls. And he was the anchor of a unit called the Doomsday Defense.

> "There isn't any use arguing with him if he gets hold of your jersey. . . . You just fall wherever Lilly wants."
>
> –Hall of Fame quarterback Bob Griese

"He is not enormous, but he is strong enough so that there isn't any use arguing with him if he gets hold of your jersey," said Hall of Fame quarterback Bob Griese. "You just fall wherever Lilly wants."

One of Griese's biggest falls was for a 29-yard loss in Super Bowl VI. Lilly and the Cowboys went on to defeat Griese's Dolphins in a 24–3 cakewalk.

Lilly brought it on every play in every game—a team-record 196 games in a row. Sacks were not an official statistic in those days, but the Cowboys claim he had 94½ of them.

"A man has to figure out what has to be done and how to do it," Lilly said. "You have to be able to spin out of a block, recognize a play immediately, and then react accordingly. I figure I am as strong as anyone else, so getting the job done becomes a matter of pride and determination."

In 1975 Lilly became the first member of the Cowboys' Ring of Honor. Five years later, he was inducted into the Pro Football Hall of Fame. And in 1994, he was named to the NFL 75th Anniversary Team. Not bad for a kid from small-town Texas.

ROGER STAUBACH (1969–1979)

Just like Lilly, quarterback Roger Staubach had a nickname that truly fit: Roger the Dodger.

He earned that nickname when he was a young scrambling quarterback. At the Naval Academy, Staubach won the Heisman Trophy–the last to do so from a military school–and then spent four years in the armed forces. He was even stationed in Vietnam for one year during the war.

In his final year of military service, Staubach had a workout with the Cowboys. He did so well that he decided he wanted to play again once left the Navy.

And play he did.

Roger Staubach scans the field during a 1976 preseason game against the Los Angeles Rams.

"Life is so short, and there are only so many chances to be in pressure situations," Staubach said. "There are only a certain number of opportunities to take your talent and ability and get things accomplished."

Staubach didn't become a starter until 1971, his third NFL season. That year, he took the Cowboys to their first Super Bowl. Dallas won 24–3 over Miami, and Staubach was the game's MVP.

In total, the Cowboys made six NFC championship games and four Super Bowls behind Staubach, winning two titles.

Staubach was known for making clutch plays both with his arm and with his feet. He was such an accurate passer that when he retired after the 1979 season, his 83.4 passer rating was highest in NFL history. He also scored 20 touchdowns on the ground.

As expected from a naval officer, Staubach was a great leader. And a great teammate.

"Teamwork has always been an important part of my life, and team players are not just people that fall into step," he said. "They're really people that have a respect for someone other than themselves and also realize that you can't get to where you want to in life by going it alone."

TONY DORSETT (1977–1987)

Running back Tony Dorsett had the perfect initials for a guy who made his living getting into the end zone: TD.

Like Staubach, Dorsett was a Heisman Trophy winner. Dorsett led the University of Pittsburgh to the national title in 1976, and he was a slam dunk to be a top selection in the 1977 NFL Draft. Dallas swung a

Tony Dorsett finds a running lane during a 1986 contest against the Rams.

trade with the Seattle Seahawks, who had the No. 2 overall pick, and just like that Dorsett was a Cowboy.

"Never had a player with this breakaway speed," coach Tom Landry said about Dorsett. "The confidence factor is going to be a big thing with a player like Dorsett. Our players know he has the ability, and there is going to be an air of confidence throughout the team about what he can do."

He could do it all. And he did.

Dorsett was the NFL's Offensive Rookie of the Year in 1977, rushing for 1,007 yards and 12 touchdowns. Dallas went on to win the Super Bowl that year, and TD even scored a TD in the game.

From there, Dorsett had seven more 1,000-yard rushing seasons. His 99-yard scoring sprint against Minnesota in 1982 remains the longest run in NFL history.

Dorsett retired with 12,739 yards rushing, 3,554 yards receiving, and 91 touchdowns. He made four Pro Bowls. For nearly his entire career, he was the one weapon opposing defenses felt they must stop.

Rarely did they.

"Before I leave, I would just like to say a big word to all those people that are out there trying to make something of themselves," Dorsett said during his 1994 Pro Football Hall of Fame induction speech. "And that is, I am good testimony that you can accomplish just about anything you want to in life . . . don't listen to other kids when they tell you, 'you cannot achieve your dreams.' Go out and set some goals for yourself, and then try to accomplish them. It is what you think of yourself that will make the biggest difference in yourself. And just remember these words: 'You can, you can, you can.'"

EMMITT SMITH (1990–2002)

Ask the other two members of the Triplets–quarterback Troy Aikman and receiver Michael Irvin–who was the most important of the three. Their answer is always the same: running back Emmitt Smith.

Smith retired as the NFL's career rushing leader, and it's a mark that still stands. Given how short running backs' careers tend to be, the record might never be broken.

Smith could do just about everything. He could block. He could run (18,355 career yards). He could catch (515 career receptions). He could score (175 career touchdowns). He made four All-Pro teams. He was selected to the Pro Bowl eight times. And he was tough.

Boy, was Emmitt Smith tough.

Never was that clearer than in the 1993 season finale at a bitterly cold Giants Stadium. The winner would take the NFC East. Smith suffered a separated shoulder late in the first half, but he refused to come out of the game. He refused to be used as a decoy. He wanted the ball.

Emmitt Smith tries to break a tackle during a game against the Giants—one of the greatest games of his career.

He got the ball. Smith ran for 168 yards to win his third consecutive NFL rushing title. The Cowboys won 16–13 in overtime.

"My memory of him from that game is what it is for his entire career," said Jason Garrett, who was the Cowboys' backup quarterback at the time and later became the team's head coach. "Emmitt was a guy you could count on at any time, but particularly in the clutch situations. Always so durable. Always so tough. Always so dependable. It was a special performance, no question about it."

THE BEST OF THE REST

TROY AIKMAN (1989–2000)

The prolific quarterback was the first pick in the Jerry Jones era—and the first overall pick in the 1989 draft. He went on to lead Dallas and the Triplets to three Super Bowls in four years.

LARRY ALLEN (1994–2005)

The powerful offensive lineman could block a runaway train. Allen was a big reason Emmitt Smith had so much success as a rusher.

BOB HAYES (1965–1974)

He was the fastest man on Earth in 1964, winning a gold medal at the Olympic Games. After that, he went on to become a Hall of Fame wide receiver. Hayes was a key member of the Cowboys team that won Super Bowl VI.

CALVIN HILL (1969–1974)

Hill was a do-everything running back who came out of the Ivy League. He helped the Cowboys win their first title in Super Bowl VI.

ED "TOO TALL" JONES (1974–1978, 1980–1989)

If you ask Jones's opponents, his nickname should have been "Too Good." The massive defensive end was a key member of the team that won Super Bowl XII.

TOM LANDRY (1960–1988)

With his stone face, fedora hat, and suit, Landry looked like a businessman. But he was the Cowboys' most successful coach. He led the team to championships in Super Bowls VI and XII.

RANDY WHITE (1975–1988)

The defensive tackle was so tough in the trenches that he was known as "the Manster." White earned co-MVP honors in Super Bowl XII.

JASON WITTEN (2003–2017)

Respected by teammates and opponents alike, Witten was one of the greatest tight ends in NFL history.

DARREN WOODSON (1992–2003)

The All-Pro safety was the boss of the defense on three Super Bowl teams in the 1990s.

TIMELINE

1960

The Dallas Cowboys debut in the NFL. The team finishes the season with a dismal record of 0–11–1.

1961

The Cowboys notch their first win in team history, beating the Steelers 27–24 in the season opener. Dallas finishes the year with a record of 4–9–1.

1964

The Cowboys select quarterback Roger Staubach in the NFL Draft, despite the fact that Staubach will have to serve four years in the military before joining the team.

1966

The Cowboys play on Thanksgiving for the first time, beating the Browns 26–14. This begins a tradition of the Cowboys playing on the holiday.

1966

The Cowboys have their first winning season (10–3–1). But on January 1, 1967, Dallas falls to the Packers 34–27 in the NFL Championship Game.

1967

After going 9–5 during the regular season, Dallas loses the NFL Championship Game to Green Bay 21–17 in a game known as the Ice Bowl.

1970

Dallas goes 10–4 during the regular season and powers its way through the playoffs. But in January 1971, the Cowboys lose their first Super Bowl 16–13 in a sloppy game against the Colts.

1971

Once again, the Cowboys have a strong regular season. And in January 1972, Dallas makes it back to the Super Bowl. With Staubach at quarterback, the Cowboys win their first title, manhandling Miami 24–3.

1975

A Hail Mary pass from Staubach to Pearson beats the Vikings in the playoffs. A few weeks later, in January 1976, the Cowboys lose to the Steelers 21–17 in Super Bowl X.

1977

The Cowboys draft Heisman Trophy–winning running back Tony Dorsett with the second overall selection. At the end of the season, Dallas wins its second Super Bowl 27–10 over Denver.

1978

Trying to defend their crown, the Cowboys go 12–4 during the regular season. But in January 1979, Dallas falls short against a powerful Steelers team and loses a classic Super Bowl 35–31.

1981

The Cowboys have another impressive regular season, going 12–4. But in January 1982, Dallas loses the NFC Championship Game to the 49ers on a play known simply as "the Catch."

1989

The Jerry Jones era begins in Dallas. Jones fires Tom Landry and hires Jimmy Johnson as head coach.

1992

The Cowboys, firing on all cylinders, go 13–3 in the regular season. And in January 1993, Dallas wins a championship with a 52–17 rout of Buffalo.

1993

After an 0–2 start to the season, the Cowboys finish strong with a record of 12–4. In January 1994, Dallas repeats as Super Bowl champion.

1995

The Triplets guide the Cowboys to a 12–4 record. In January 1996, Dallas defeats Pittsburgh in Super Bowl XXX. With the victory, the Cowboys become the first team to win three Super Bowls in four years.

2009

Cowboys Stadium, later called AT&T Stadium, opens in Arlington. The Cowboys lose their first game in the stadium to the New York Giants.

2014

Tony Romo leads the Cowboys to an impressive 12–4 record. But in the playoffs, Dallas loses to Green Bay after a controversial ruling on a Dez Bryant no-catch.

2016

Rookie sensation Dak Prescott guides the Cowboys to a 13–3 record. However, Dallas loses a heartbreaker to Green Bay in the playoffs.

COWBOYS RECORDS

ALL-TIME RECORD

502–374–6

PLAYOFF RECORD

34–27

SUPER BOWL RECORD

5–3

CAREER PASSING LEADER

Tony Romo: 34,183 yards; 248 TDs

CAREER RUSHING LEADER

Emmitt Smith: 17,162 yards; 153 TDs

CAREER RECEIVING LEADER

Jason Witten: 12,448 yards; 68 TDs

CAREER SCORING LEADER

Emmitt Smith: 986 points

CAREER SACKS LEADER

DeMarcus Ware: 117 sacks

CAREER INTERCEPTIONS LEADER

Mel Renfro: 52 interceptions

WINNINGEST COACH

Tom Landry: 250–162–6

** Accurate through the 2017 season.*

FOR MORE INFORMATION

BOOKS

Aron, Jaime. *So You Think You're a Dallas Cowboys Fan? Stars, Stats, Records, and Memories for True Diehards.* New York: Sports Publishing, 2016.

Reeves, Jim. *Dallas Cowboys: The Legends of America's Team.* Fort Worth, TX: Berkeley Place Books, 2017.

Wilner, Barry. *Troy Aikman and the Dallas Cowboys.* Minneapolis: Abdo Publishing, 2018.

ON THE WEB

Dallas Cowboys
www.dallascowboys.com

National Football League
www.nfl.com

Pro Football Hall of Fame
www.profootballhof.com

PLACES TO VISIT

AT&T STADIUM

1 AT&T Way
Arlington, TX 76011
817-892-4000
www.attstadium.com

Originally called Cowboys Stadium and forever known as Jerry World, it's one of the most impressive venues in sports.

PRO FOOTBALL HALL OF FAME

2121 George Halas Dr. NW
Canton, OH 44708
330-456-8207
www.profootballhof.com

The Hall of Fame is a museum dedicated to football. There are exhibits on the origin of the game, artifacts from famous moments, and busts honoring the greatest players and coaches ever.

SELECT BIBLIOGRAPHY

Archer, Todd. "Jerry Jones Talks Tom Landry Firing." ESPN, 23 Feb. 2014, www.espn.com/dallas/nfl/story/_/id/10507538/jerry-jones-dallas-cowboys-says-regrets-firing-tom-landry.

Badenhausen, Kurt. "The Cowboys and Yankees Top the World's Most Valuable Sports Teams of 2017." *Forbes*, 12 July 2017, www.forbes.com/sites/kurtbadenhausen/2017/07/12/the-cowboys-and-yankees-top-the-worlds-most-valuable-sports-teams-of-2017/#2c1c08b35018.

Banks, Don. "The Botch Heard 'Round the World: Revisiting Romo's Gaffe in Seattle." *Sports Illustrated*, 8 Oct. 2014, www.si.com/nfl/2014/10/08/tony-romo-dallas-cowboys-seattle-seahawks-bill-parcells-mike-holmgren.

"Dallas Cowboys Franchise Encyclopedia." *Pro Football Reference*, www.pro-football-reference.com/teams/dal/index.htm. Accessed 4 Oct. 2018.

Farmer, Sam. "Drew Pearson Recalls the First Hail Mary Pass." *Los Angeles Times*, 25 Dec. 2014, www.latimes.com/sports/nfl/la-sp-hail-mary-drew-pearson-20141226-story.html.

Hill, Clarence E., Jr. "Gil Brandt, the Godfather of Scouting, Is Right at Home with Draft at AT&T Stadium." *Fort Worth Star-Telegram*, 25 Apr. 2018, www.star-telegram.com/sports/nfl/dallas-cowboys/article209855084.html.

Moore, David. "In Most Courageous Game, Emmitt Smith Overcame Injury to Carry Cowboys." *SportsDay*, 6 Aug. 2010, sportsday.dallasnews.com/dallas-cowboys/emmittsmith/2010/08/06/in-most-courageous-game-emmitt-smith-overcame-injury-to-carry-cowboys.

Myers, Gary. "Cowboys' Jerry Jones Opens Up to News about Trying to End Super Bowl Drought, Tony Romo, Dak Prescott, and Possible HoF Election." *New York Daily News*, 10 Dec. 2016, www.nydailynews.com/sports/football/jerry-jones-opens-super-bowl-drought-article-1.2906110.

Parziale, James. "Michael Irvin's Career Ended against Eagles – And Their Fans Cheered." *Fox Sports*, 17 Sept. 2015, www.foxsports.com/nfl/laces-out/story/dallas-cowboys-michael-irvin-career-ended-philadelphia-eagles-tbt-091715.

Redmond, Lisa. "Three Years Later, the NFL Now Says Cowboys' Dez Bryant Did, in Fact, Catch It." *NBC Sports Washington*, 28 Feb. 2018, www.nbcsports.com/washington/redskins/three-years-later-nfl-now-says-cowboys-dez-bryant-did-fact-catch-it.

INDEX

ABOUT THE AUTHOR

Barry Wilner has been a sportswriter for the Associated Press since 1976. He is the AP's national pro football writer and has covered every Super Bowl since 1987. Barry also has authored 67 books. He lives in Garnerville, New York.